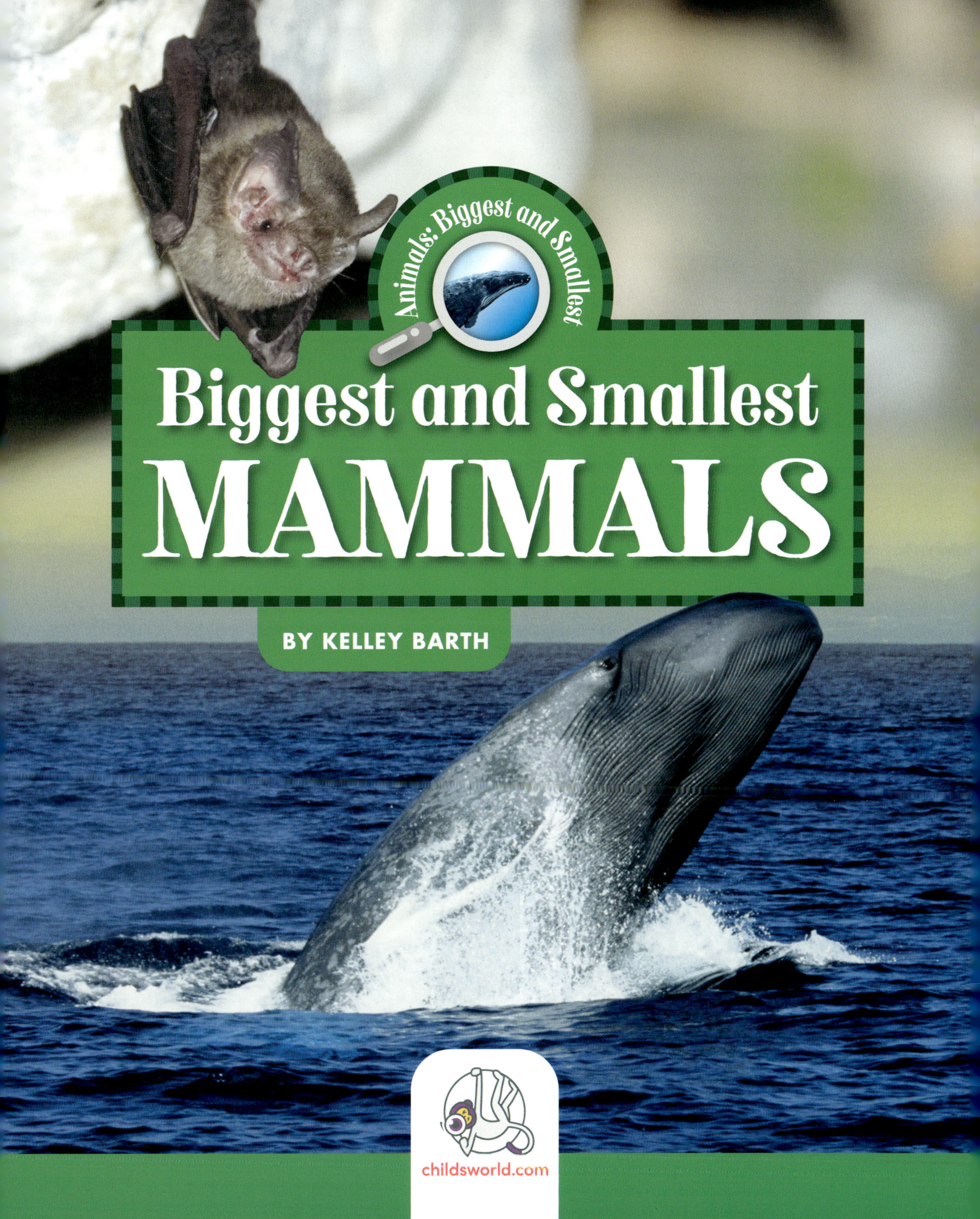
Animals: Biggest and Smallest
Biggest and Smallest
MAMMALS
BY KELLEY BARTH
childsworld.com

Published by The Child's World®
800-599-READ • childsworld.com

Photography Credits
Cover: ©arthur_ensis/iNaturalist; ©Gerard Soury/The Image Bank/Getty Images; ©Gulf MG/Shutterstock; ©danbrownnature/iNaturalist; page 2: ©Gulf MG/Shutterstock; page 3: ©Dorling Kindersley/Dorling Kindersley RF/Getty Images; page 5: ©Amarisa M/Shutterstock; page 5: ©Gerard Soury/The Image Bank/Getty Images; page 6–7: ©eco2drew/iStock/Getty Images; page 8: ©Gerald Corsi/iStock/Getty Images; page 8–9: ©Gerard Soury/The Image Bank/Getty Images; page 10: ©MerlinTuttle.org/Science Source; page 13: ©arthur_ensis/iNaturalist; page 14–15: ©Design_Lands/Shutterstock; page 15: ©kdshutterman/iStock/Getty Images; page 15: ©Mr. Beekeeper/Shutterstock; page 16: ©Drp8/Shutterstock; page 18–19: ©Grilleau Nicolas/iStock/Getty Images; page 19: ©arthur_ensis/iNaturalist; page 22: ©Michael Burrell/iStock/Getty Images; page 22: ©NatashaBo/iStock/Getty Images

ISBN Information
9781503875623 (Reinforced Library Binding)
9781503876163 (Portable Document Format)
9781503876781 (Online Multi-user eBook)
9781503877283 (Electronic Publication)

LCCN
2025938250

Printed in the United States of America

ABOUT THE AUTHOR

Kelley Barth is the author of over a dozen books for children. She is also a mammal who is bigger than a bumblebee bat but smaller than a blue whale. When she isn't busy writing, she enjoys reading, hiking, crafting, and going on adventures with her husband and son.

Table of Contents

Mammals Big and Small

Big, small, and in between, mammals live on every continent in the world. Mammals come in many shapes and sizes. They live in oceans and deserts, high up in the trees, and underground. All mammals have a backbone and are **warm-blooded**. All mammals have some type of hair, even if only a tiny bit. Most mammals don't lay eggs. Instead, they give birth and **nurse** their young.

If you are lucky, you may catch a glimpse of a blue whale swimming through the ocean. It is the biggest mammal in the world. Deep in a cave in Asia lives the bumblebee bat. It is the smallest mammal in the world. These animals look very different from each other. But what do they have in common?

Bats are the only mammals that can fly.

Blue whales are one of many mammals that live in water.

Blue whales are surprisingly fast swimmers. They can go up to 30 miles (48.3 kilometers) per hour.

Where Do Blue Whales Live?

Meet the Blue Whale!

Blue whales aren't just the biggest mammal. They are the biggest animal that has ever lived. They are even larger than every dinosaur that ever lived! Blue whales are around 100 feet (30.5 meters) long. They are longer than a basketball court, or almost three school buses. Blue whales are heavy, too. These giants weigh up to 400,000 pounds (181,436.9 kilograms), or 200 tons. That is about the size of a house or an airplane! Even a blue whale's tongue is heavy. It weighs as much as an elephant.

Blue whales live in every ocean except for the Arctic Ocean. Thick layers of **blubber** help their large bodies float.

Being big isn't always easy. Big animals have big appetites. Blue whales eat only krill. Krill are one of the smallest animals in the ocean. So blue whales need to eat a lot. A blue whale eats millions of krill in a single day! In order to eat, a blue whale swallows a big gulp of water and krill. Then, it filters the water back out of its mouth through a special material called **baleen**.

Blue whales also need lots of food to support their organs. Their hearts are almost the size of a large motorcycle!

A single krill is only around 2 or 3 inches (5.1–7.6 centimeters) long.

GIANTS OF THE OCEAN

One reason blue whales are as big as they are is because they live in the ocean. The salty ocean water helps support their huge size. On land, **gravity** would pull them down. Big land animals need big legs for support. And a blue whale would need huge legs to support its weight. Such legs would be too heavy to walk!

Blue whales are gentle and do not attack humans.

THE ETRUSCAN SHREW

The bumblebee bat isn't alone in the "smallest mammal" category. The Etruscan shrew weighs even less than the bumblebee bat. It is the smallest mammal by weight. But the shrew's body is about 1 inch (2.5 cm) longer than the bat's.

Bumblebee bats are also called Kitti's hog-nosed bats because of their pig-like snout.

Meet the Bumblebee Bat!

There isn't anything big about the bumblebee bat. This teeny, tiny mammal could rest on your thumb. It is also called a Kitti's hog-nosed bat. Many people call it a bumblebee bat because it is no bigger than a bumblebee! The bumblebee bat measures just over 1 inch (2.5 cm) from top to bottom. It only weighs 0.07 ounces (2 grams). That is the same weight as two paper clips!

Bumblebee bats only live in one small area of the world. They **roost** in caves along the border between the countries of Thailand and Myanmar.

It doesn't take much to fill up such a small stomach. Bumblebee bats hunt for food twice a day. They are active for about 20 minutes at dawn and 30 minutes in the evening. The bats spend the rest of the time inside their cave. Bumblebee bats usually eat as they fly. They hover above treetops and gulp down small insects and spiders.

Where Do Bumblebee Bats Live?

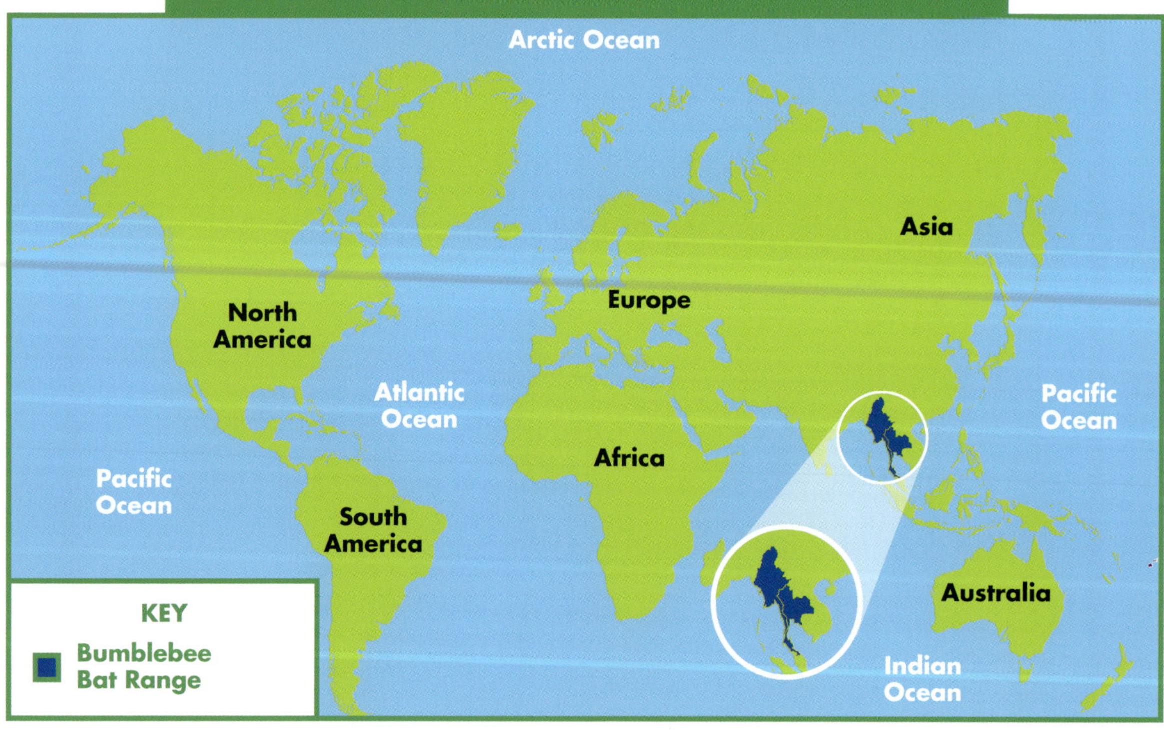

Bumblebee bats live in groups, but they usually hunt and eat alone.

How They Compare

Blue whales are 90 million times heavier than bumblebee bats. Even though they are very different sizes, these animals share an **ancestor**. Scientists believe that all mammals **evolved** from the same animal. It lived around 200 million years ago and looked like a small shrew. Over time, blue whales grew larger and larger. Bumblebee bats shrank to their tiny size. Wings that fly and flippers that swim may look very different on the outside. But on the inside, the bones of a whale, a bat, and even a human look pretty similar!

MEASURING UP

A fully grown bumblebee bat would fit easily inside your pocket, but even a baby blue whale is already four times longer and weighs 25 times more than an adult human!

Bumblebee bat
Weight: 0.07 ounces (2 g)
Height: 1 inch (2.5 cm)

10-year-old-child
Weight: 70.5 pounds (32 kg)
Height: 55 inches (1.4 m)

Blue whale
Weight: 400,000 pounds (181,436.9 kg)
Length: 100 feet (30.5 m)

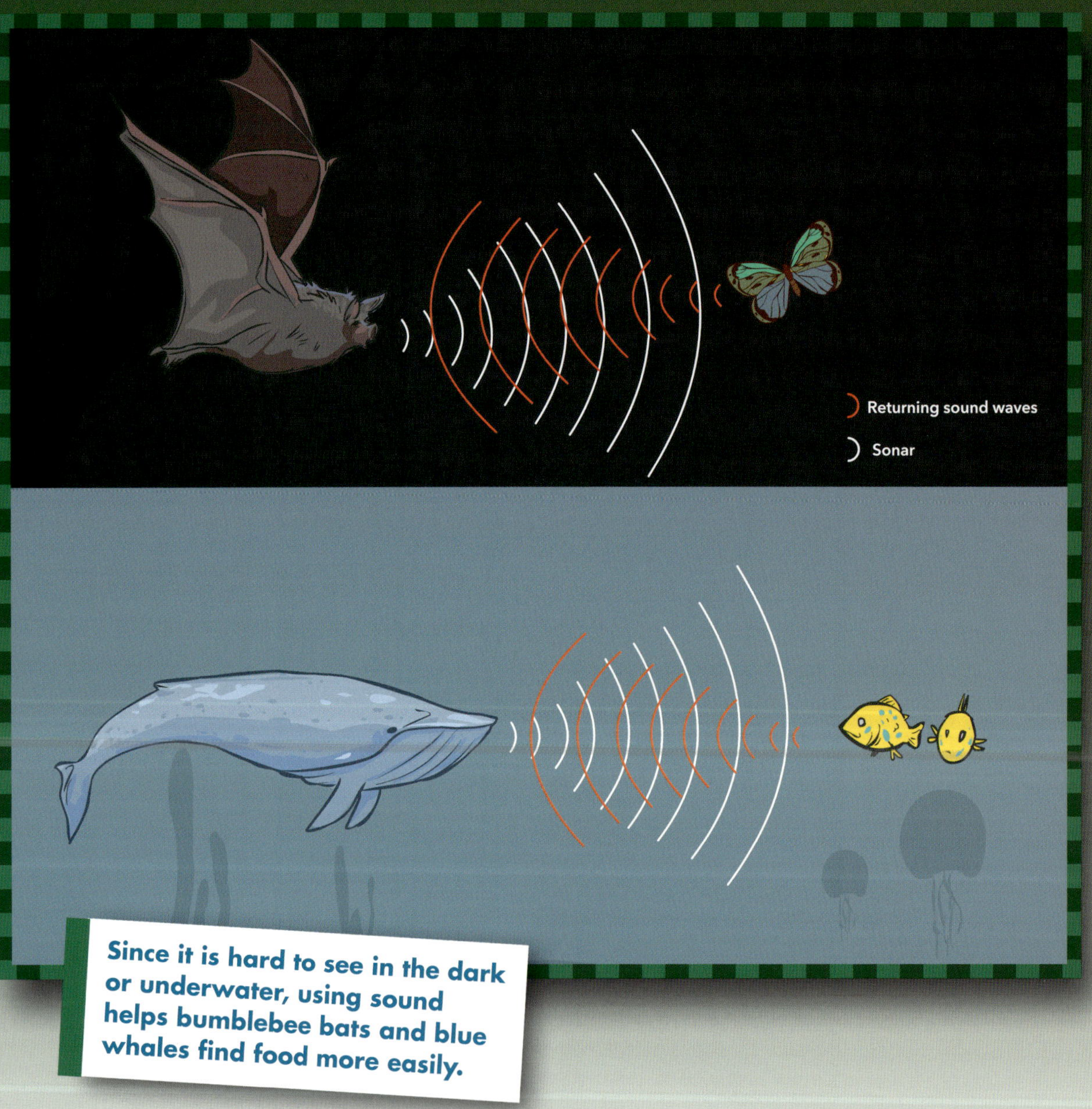

Since it is hard to see in the dark or underwater, using sound helps bumblebee bats and blue whales find food more easily.

Their size isn't the only big thing about blue whales. The noises they make are also big. They are one of loudest animals on Earth. Blue whales are thought to be able to hear each other's calls from 1,000 miles (1,609.3 km) away. Scientists think their loud noises might also work like **sonar**. Sonar uses sound waves so the whales can measure distance. The noise of their loud calls bounces back and helps them avoid objects as they travel underwater.

Bumblebee bats use **echolocation**, which is similar to sonar. A bat makes a sound and waits to hear the sound's echo. Based on how the echo sounds, a bumblebee bat can tell where an object is in the air. This helps the bats hunt for insects as they fly.

Family life is important for both whales and bats. Bumblebee bats give birth to one pup each spring. The new pups nurse until they are strong enough to fly and hunt.

Blue whales give birth every two to three years. Whale calves drink their mother's milk for around seven months. During their first year, blue whale calves gain about 200 pounds (90.7 kg) every day!

Bumblebee bats live in groups of around 100 animals. Most blue whales live alone or in small groups of two to three. However, larger groups can form when the whales **migrate** to new waters.

Bumblebee bats have unique feet that grasp automatically when they hang upside down to sleep.

STRANGE SLEEPERS

These mammals have some odd sleep habits. Bumblebee bats sleep hanging upside down in their caves. Most bats' legs wouldn't be strong enough to support their bodies if they slept upright. Blue whales only sleep with half of their brain resting at a time! The other half stays awake to help them swim and breathe.

A baby blue whale is about the size of a school bus.

The Big and Small Future

Blue whales and bumblebee bats have one other important thing in common. There is still so much we don't know about them! It can be hard to study these animals. They are fairly rare. There are fewer than 25,000 blue whales alive today. Scientists think there are probably fewer than 10,000 bumblebee bats. Scientists try to find ways to learn more without harming the animals or their **habitats**. There is a lot we don't know about their lives or behaviors. But even the smallest details can help us make big discoveries.

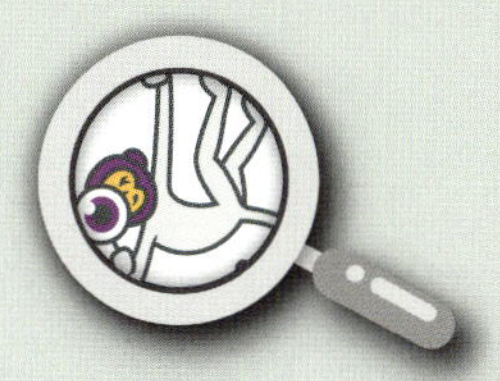

WONDER MORE

Wondering About New Information:

What did you learn about blue whales and bumblebee bats? Write down three new facts you learned. Did this information surprise you? Why or why not?

Wondering How It Matters:

How is an animal's size important? What are some good things about being big? What are some good things about being small?

Wondering Why:

What do blue whales and bumblebee bats have in common? Why are their similarities and differences important?

Ways to Keep Wondering:

After reading this book, what questions do you have about blue whales and bumblebee bats? What can you do to learn more about them?

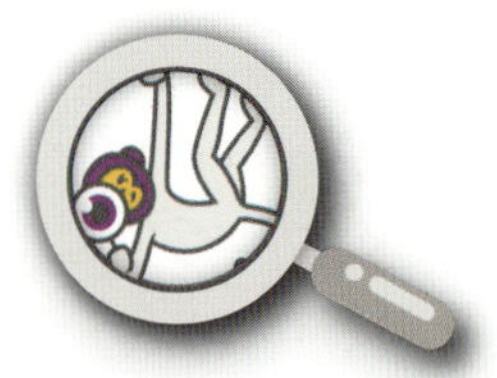

SAME AND DIFFERENT

How are blue whales and bumblebee bats the same? How are they different? It's your turn to design a photo display about these two amazing mammals.

Supplies

- paper plates
- glue
- scissors
- old magazines and photos

Directions

1 Glue two paper plates together, overlapping with about half of one plate on top of the other (to create a Venn diagram).

2 Add titles so one plate is for the blue whale, one is for the bumblebee bat, and the overlapping part is for both.

3 Look for pictures to cut out that representative of one or both animals. Think about what they eat, where they live, and what they look like. For example, can you find pictures of the ocean or caves?

4 Add the pictures under the correct section (whale, bat, or both).

5 Feel free to get creative and draw your own pictures as well. This is a great way to see the similarities and differences between these two animals.

GLOSSARY

ancestor (AN-ses-stur) An ancestor is a relative from a very long time ago.

baleen (buh-LEEN) Baleen hangs down in a whale's mouth and helps them filter food.

blubber (BLUH-bur) Blubber is the fat that helps keep whales warm.

echolocation (ek-oh-low-KAY-shun) Echolocation allows animals to locate objects based on the echo of their sound waves.

evolved (ee-VOLVD) A plant or animal that has evolved has changed over time.

gravity (GRA-vuh-tee) Gravity is the force that pulls objects to the ground.

habitat (HA-buh-tat) A habitat is the place where an animal lives.

migrate (MY-grayt) Migrate means to move from one place to another.

nurse (NURS) Mother animals nurse their young with their own milk.

roost (ROOST) Bats roost where they settle down to rest or sleep.

sonar (SOH-nar) Sonar uses sound waves to locate objects and find distances.

warm-blooded (warm-BLUD-ed) Warm-blooded animals are able to hold their body temperature steady throughout different weather conditions.

FIND OUT MORE

In the Library

Brown, Kendra. *Small but Mighty: Why Earth's Tiny Creatures Matter.* Toronto, Ontario, CAN: Owlkids Books, 2021.

Maloney, Brenna. *Mammals.* New York, NY: Children's Press, 2023.

Regan, Lisa, and Patrick Corrigan. *How Big?: Animals.* London, UK: Arcturus, 2024.

On the Web

Visit our website for links about the biggest and smallest mammals:
childsworld.com/links

Note to Parents, Caregivers, Teachers, and Librarians: We routinely verify our web links to make sure they are safe and active sites. So encourage your readers to check them out!

INDEX